22.88

402495

9/03

AROUND THE WORLD IN...

800

AROUND THE WORLD IN...

800

by Linda S. George

BENCHMARK BOOKS

MARSHALL CAVENDISH
NEW YORK

With thanks to J. Brett McClain of the Oriental Institute,
the University of Chicago, for his careful reading of the manuscript

For Richard

• • •

Benchmark Books
Marshall Cavendish
99 White Plains Road
Tarrytown, New York 10591-9001
www.marshallcavendish.com

• • •

Library of Congress Cataloging-in-Publication Data
George, Linda S., 1949–
800/Linda S. George.
p. cm—(Around the world in—)
Includes bibliographical references and index.
ISBN 0-7614-1085-6 (lib. bdg.)
1. Eight hundred, A.D.—Juvenile literature.   2. Eighth century—Juvenile literature.
3. Ninth century—Juvenile literature.
[1. Eight hundred, A.D. 2. Middle Ages—History. 3. World history.]
I. Title. II. Series.
Summary: Surveys important occurrences in Europe, Africa, Asia and the Americas around the year 800.
CB353.8 .G46 2001   909.07—dc21   00-050758

• • •

Printed in Italy
1 3 5 6 4 2

• • •

Book Designer: Judith Turziano
Photo Research: Rose Corbett Gordon, Mystic CT

• • •

half title: Charlemagne, with Pope Leo III to his right and a bishop to his left.
title page: *Left*: A landscape painted on silk by LiSixun during the Tang dynasty.
Right: A portrait of Saint Matthew from the Lindisfarne Gospels.

• • •

CONTENTS

Charlemagne, king of the Franks, built a great empire in western Europe and encouraged the spread of learning and the arts.

INTRODUCTION

The year is 800. In Europe Viking longboats prowl the seas, while two powerful rulers—one Christian, one Muslim—are building vibrant outposts of learning and culture. Far to the east, China's Tang dynasty presides over a golden age of art and poetry. North Africa is home to a magnificent Muslim mosque, while traders to West Africa describe the empire of Ghana as a "land of gold." In the Americas giant earthen pyramids and great stone temples stand as monuments to the all-powerful gods.

If you could board a time machine and go back to the year 800, these are some of the things you might witness. Most people learn about history by focusing on just one country or place. Usually they learn about events only from their own perspective, that is, from the point of view of their nation or heritage. This is certainly a valid way to try to understand the world, but it can also be narrow and one-sided. In this book we thought it might be interesting to take a different approach to history, by looking at events that were occurring all across the world at one period of time. Perhaps if we take this broader, "bird's-eye" view of history, all of us may be able to understand one another a little better.

So step aboard our "time machine," and get ready to take a trip around the world.

EUROPE AROUND 800

GREENLAND

ICELAND

NORWAY

North Sea

SWEDEN

Baltic Sea

DENMARK

SCOTLAND

LINDISFARNE

York

IRELAND
Dublin

ENGLAND
London

Aix-la-Chapelle

English Channel

Rhine River

NORMANDY

Seine River

Paris

Atlantic Ocean

Pyrenees

Rome

Black Sea

Constantinople

GREECE

Mediterranean Sea

AL-ANDALUS
Córdoba

Strait of Gibraltar
Ceuta

SYRIA

Damascus

Euphrates River

Baghdad

PALESTINE

EGYPT

Mecca

◼ MUSLIM SPAIN
◼ THE FRANKISH EMPIRE
◼ BYZANTINE EMPIRE

Miles 0   200   500
Kilometers 0   400   800

PART I

EUROPE

In Europe around the year 800, people were on the move—exploring the seas and invading neighboring lands, amassing great libraries and building great kingdoms. On the ruins of the ancient Roman world, Charlemagne was founding a new empire. Meanwhile, fearsome Viking warriors were raiding Europe's coastal settlements and river cities. In Spain, a fugitive Arab prince was building a splendid capital that would become known as the "jewel of the world."

WHEN THEY RULED

The Carolingian Dynasty
639–843

The Irish Monastery Period
431–875

The Viking Age
c. 790–1100

The Umayyad Dynasty in Spain
756–1031

THE FRANKS
CHARLEMAGNE SETS THINGS STRAIGHT

It was nearing Christmas in the year 800, and Pope Leo III, head of the Christian church in Rome, was in trouble. His enemies had tried to put out his eyes and cut out his tongue, and he needed a protector. Charlemagne, king of the Franks—the peoples who lived in modern-day France and Germany —appeared to be the man for the job. Known as a great warrior, Charlemagne had conquered much of Europe, bringing the Lombards of northern Italy, most of the tribes of France, and the fierce Saxons of Germany under his control. Under his leadership, much of western Europe was united as a single powerful kingdom.

Charlemagne had journeyed to Rome that winter to "set in order the affairs of the Church, which were in great confusion."* As the king knelt in prayer in the church of Saint Peter on Christmas Day, Pope Leo made his way through the crowd and stood in front of the celebrated warrior. People looked on in astonishment as the pope placed a crown on Charlemagne's head and declared him Roman emperor.

The pope had just done something very bold and dangerous. Popes did not crown Roman emperors—that title was not the pope's to give. Instead the title belonged to the emperor of the Byzantine Empire, whose capital was in Constantinople, the city now known as Istanbul, Turkey.

Constantinople and Rome had been rivals for centuries. Until the early fourth century, the Roman Empire had been centered in Rome. But in the year 330, the Roman emperor Constantine I, who had converted to Christianity, moved the capital from Rome to the Greek city of

* These are the words of Einhard, Charlemagne's biographer. See "Just How Tall *Was* Charlemagne?" on page 16 for more about this fascinating source of information.

Charlemagne was not always victorious. Here he is depicted battling Muslim armies in Spain in 778. Charlemagne's army was forced to retreat across the Pyrenees, and his men suffered great hardship. That retreat was immortalized in the famous French poem The Song of Roland.

Byzantium. He renamed the city after himself, calling it Constantinople. The western half of the empire—the part still centered in Rome— collapsed in the fifth century when Rome fell to barbarian tribes. Meanwhile, the eastern half—known as the Byzantine Empire—thrived. In the eighth century Rome once again rose to importance as the center

of the powerful Catholic Church. The Catholic popes in Rome often came into conflict with the Byzantine emperor in Constantinople.

In the year 800 the Byzantine Empire was in a particularly troubled state. Its leader was not only weak and cruel, but she was also a woman. In 797 Irene had taken the title of empress after having her son, the rightful heir

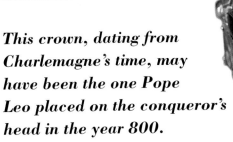

Pope Leo III crowns Charlemagne Roman emperor in this painting made some centuries after the event. Charlemagne was so popular a ruler that his exploits and accomplishments live on to this day.

to the throne, blinded. Pope Leo might have overlooked Irene's cruelty, but he just could not accept the idea of a female ruler. To him, a woman on the throne meant an empty throne. Accordingly, he felt free to crown his own candidate, Charlemagne.

Charlemagne took Christianity very seriously. He had built a beautiful church at his capital, Aix-la-Chapelle (akes-lah-shah-PELL), also known as Aachen

This crown, dating from Charlemagne's time, may have been the one Pope Leo placed on the conqueror's head in the year 800.

WHAT YEAR IS THIS, ANYWAY?

The calendar used in much of the world today—the calendar that calculates years in terms of B.C. (before Christ) and A.D. (*anno Domini*, Latin for "in the year of the Lord")—was invented by a monk named Dionysius Exiguus in the sixth century. Up until that time (and even after), all the Christian churches couldn't agree on when to begin and end the year, and how to calculate when holidays such as Easter should be celebrated.

Many Christians agreed that the birth of Jesus Christ would be a good date from which to start calculating time. Since no one knew the exact date of Jesus' birth, Dionysius came up with a logical solution. There were lists of Roman emperors and the years they had ruled, beginning with Rome's founding. From these lists, Dionysius calculated when Christ was born by figuring out when Herod, the Roman who ruled Palestine at the time of Jesus, was king.

By the time of Charlemagne, Dionysius's calendar was accepted by most Christians in Europe. In other parts of the world, though, the year 800 was not 800 at all. The Muslims in the Middle East, North Africa, and Spain had their own way of counting the years. So did the Jews, Hindus, Chinese, Maya, and everybody else who was not part of the Christian world.

(AH-kun), near the Rhine River, and he worshipped there several times a day. He gave generously not only to the poor in his own kingdom, but also to needy Christians in Syria, Egypt, and North Africa. He had a special love for the church of Saint Peter in Rome and, as his biographer Einhard

Charlemagne may be best remembered for his encouragement of learning. This illustration of a scribe hard at work is from a manuscript copied during Charlemagne's time.

JUST HOW TALL WAS CHARLEMAGNE?

We know quite a lot about Charlemagne—what he looked like, how he treated his children, what he enjoyed doing—thanks largely to a monk named Einhard. Einhard was born around 770 and arrived at Charlemagne's court in 791 or 792. He served Charlemagne until the king's death in 814 and wrote the biography of his patron a few years later.

Charlemagne was widely admired and respected, and Einhard's *Life of Charlemagne*, written in Latin, was very popular. The manuscript was copied many times. About eighty copies survive, some dating from the ninth and tenth centuries. Even today this little book is popular. You can read a translation and find out such interesting facts as how tall Charlemagne was ("his height is well known to have been seven times the length of his foot"), what he liked to eat ("roasts"), and how he raised his children ("he was so careful of training of his sons and daughters that he never took his meals without them when he was at home").

related, he "heaped its treasury with a vast wealth of gold, silver, and precious stones." He also sent generous gifts to the popes, which no doubt weighed in Pope Leo's decision to crown him Roman emperor.

Charlemagne lived at a time when most people in Europe could not read or write—a period commonly known as the Dark Ages. After Rome had fallen to barbarian tribes in the 400s, European society had been plunged into chaos. People worried about survival and had little energy left to devote to the finer aspects of living. But the picture of this period as a time of darkness and lack of progress is not entirely accurate. There

Einhard, Charlemagne's biographer

were many outposts of learning and culture, and Charlemagne himself presided over one of them.

Charlemagne had great respect for learning. He studied Latin, the language used by scholars in Europe during the Middle Ages, and "could speak it as well as his native tongue." He also studied Greek, rhetoric (the art of speaking effectively), and astronomy, which was essential for travelers. He tried to write, too, but never quite got the hang of it. Einhard tells us that Charlemagne kept tablets "in bed under his pillow, that at leisure hours he might accustom his hand to form

HAVE A CHEESE SANDWICH FOR CHARLEMAGNE

In 774 Charlemagne had just defeated the Lombards, the Germanic rulers of northern Italy, and was on his way back home to Aix-la-Chapelle. He stopped on the Plateau de Brie, east of Paris, near a monastery called the Abbey of Meaux. It was Lent, the period before Easter when Christians practice self-denial and avoid eating meat. The monks of the abbey offered Charlemagne a plate with a round cheese on it, instead of meat. They told him to eat the entire cheese, including the velvety white rind. He did and he loved it. He ordered two batches of this cheese, called Brie, to be sent to Aix-la-Chapelle every year.

Brie is still a very popular cheese, and many supermarkets carry it. You can buy a wedge of Brie and make yourself a sandwich in honor of Charlemagne. You should refrigerate the cheese until an hour or so before you plan to eat it. Take the cheese out of the refrigerator and let it sit until it reaches room temperature and softens. Then cut it into thin wedges, as if you were cutting a pie. Brie is especially good between slices of crusty French bread and would make a perfect sandwich for a school lunch. Make the sandwich with the cold cheese right out of the refrigerator; by lunchtime the Brie will be soft and—well—aromatic. If your classmates wonder who's got the smelly sneakers, just tell them you're remembering Charlemagne!

the letters," but his efforts "met with ill success."

To encourage the spread of knowledge, Charlemagne established the Palatine School at Aix-la-Chapelle and hired the most renowned scholar of his day, the monk Alcuin, to run it. Charlemagne collected manuscripts from all over Europe. These contained the works of ancient Greek and Roman scholars. Alcuin oversaw the process of having the manuscripts copied and illustrated. The pages of these books were secured in expensive bindings, often made of carved ivory encrusted with jewels. The splendid books were then sent as presents to important people all over Europe.

What mattered most, though, about the books was not their monetary value but the fact that they were copied at all. When the monks at the Palatine School copied a manuscript, they ensured that the knowledge of the ancients would survive.

The growth of art, architecture, scholarship, and learning under Charlemagne is known as the Carolingian Renaissance. (*Carol* was the Frankish name for Charlemagne, and *renaissance* means "rebirth.") An important feature of this artistic and intellectual rebirth was the system of writing developed by Charlemagne's scribes—a clear, elegant, easy-to-read script called Carolingian. Charlemagne died in 814, and his renaissance did not continue for long after. But the foundation for the western Europe we know today had been laid during his reign.

THE IRISH

A RAY OF LIGHT IN THE "DARK AGES"

It was not only Charlemagne who helped pass on the knowledge of the ancient world. In Ireland, for hundred of years, monks had been carefully copying ancient texts. Alcuin, head of Charlemagne's Palatine School, had studied under Irish monks, who were regarded as the greatest intellectuals of the time. The Irish traced their origins to the Celts (kelts). Celtic tribes had first appeared in central Europe more than 1,200 years earlier. By the fifth century B.C., they dominated the continent. Constantly fighting one another, constantly seeking

Irish monks created some of the most beautiful manuscripts ever produced, filled with intricate illustrations and elegant lettering. But Irish scribes were also masters of simplicity. They devised an alphabet of simple letters that were easy to write and to read, called Irish minuscule, and this became the common script of the Middle Ages.

It's a Monk's Life

Monks are men who separate themselves from the world in order to lead a religious life. From about the fifth century on, monasteries—communities for these men—were built all over Europe. (There were convents, or nunneries, for women.) Life inside the monastery walls was strictly regulated according to principles, or rules. The Rule of Saint Benedict was followed in many monasteries.

Saint Benedict's regulations covered every aspect of life, from how beds should be arranged to how kitchen chores should be performed to punishment for those who disobeyed. Days were filled with activity, as Saint Benedict regarded idleness as the "enemy of the soul." Monks spent many of their waking hours in prayer. They were "to obey any command of a superior as if it were a command of God."

Besides growing and preparing food, monks also worked at copying books, including religious texts, the classic works of authors such as Virgil and Ovid, and scientific texts. A special room, the scriptorium, was set aside for copying. Every book had to be handwritten on parchment, an expensive sheet made from animal skin. Some books were elaborately illustrated with paints made of gold and other precious materials. Monasteries often had extensive libraries, and monks were widely respected as men of learning.

new lands, they made their way farther and farther west, crossing the seas to what is now the British Isles. Then, in the fifth century A.D., Germanic tribes—the Angles, Saxons, and Jutes—invaded England and pushed the Celts living there to the edges of the isles—to present-day Ireland, Scotland,

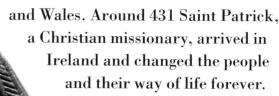

and Wales. Around 431 Saint Patrick, a Christian missionary, arrived in Ireland and changed the people and their way of life forever. He converted the Celts to Christianity. Monasteries soon sprang up all over Ireland and places nearby. One of these monasteries was located on Lindisfarne, a beautiful and isolated island off the coast of northern England. By 790, Lindisfarne had long been a center of learning. It was full of treasures, including beautifully decorated copies of the Bible. But in 793 new invaders burst onto the scene. *The Anglo-Saxon Chronicle*, a book written to record each year's events, described what happened that year: "On the sixth of the Ides of June the ravaging of the heathen men lamentably destroyed God's church at Lindisfarne."

The Vikings had arrived.

We can imagine the chilling scene: a Viking longboat gliding onto the pebbly

This bishop's staff, now in Sweden, originally came from an Irish monastery. It was most likely taken to Sweden by Vikings who had raided the Irish coast.

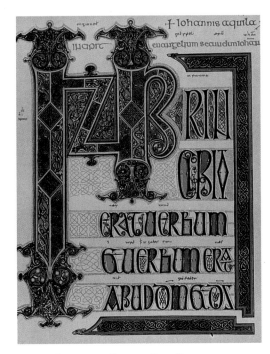

The treasured pages, copied with such painstaking care and artistry, merited nothing less than a binding set with jewels and precious metal. This binding once held the Lindisfarne Gospels.

A page from the famous Lindisfarne Gospels, copied by a scribe named Eadfrith around the year 700. The jewel-like colors and the astonishing detail make it easy to see why Irish manuscripts were so highly prized.

beach at Lindisfarne, forty or fifty warriors charging out, their weapons clanging. The Vikings killed many of the monks and took others to be sold as slaves. The brutal attack shocked Christian Europe, but it was only the beginning. Over the next seventy years, the Vikings revisited the monastery several times, torturing and killing the monks and setting the buildings on fire. In 875 the survivors finally gave up in despair and left Lindisfarne.

THE VIKINGS
LONGBOATS SET SAIL

Who were the Vikings, the "heathen men" who ravaged Lindisfarne?
The Vikings were warriors from the Scandinavian countries of Denmark,
Norway, and Sweden who lived from the late 700s until the mid-1000s.
No one is entirely sure about the original meaning of the word *Viking*.
It may be related to *vik*, which means "saltwater inlet" or "creek" in Old
Norse, the language the early Scandinavians spoke. The Vikings were also
called Norsemen—"men from the north." The people who lived along
Europe's rivers and coasts feared the Vikings as merciless pirates. But the
Vikings did more than raid and pillage. They eventually established
colonies—in Greenland and Iceland, for example—and built trading posts.

The Vikings began to venture out into the open waters of the Baltic and
North Seas at the end of the 700s, after they had perfected the longboat.
Made of overlapping oak planks and set with a square woolen sail, the
Viking longboat was light and quick. With its prow carved into the shape
of a dragon or fierce bird, it glided through the water, its frame so supple
that it flexed with the waves. Guided by oars, the longboat could put into
shore quickly and attack before the inhabitants knew what was happening.
The boats were also light enough to be carried overland.

Longboats could not only navigate the open seas, they could also sail up
shallow inland waters. In the early 800s the Vikings sailed into the heartland
of Russia and then traveled south to trade with merchants in Baghdad,
the great trading center in what is now Iraq. In 886 Viking longboats made
their way up the Seine River in France and threatened Paris. The northwest
coastal region of France is still called Normandy, after the Norsemen who
controlled it in the tenth century.

The Viking longboat was a vessel of elegance and beauty, but it also struck fear into the hearts of the people whose lands the Norsemen ravaged.

By the tenth century the Vikings also controlled nearly half of England. In the city of York, where they settled and prospered, archaeologists have uncovered such unwarlike artifacts as combs, clothing, and ice skates with blades of bone. During the eleventh century—five hundred years before Christopher Columbus—a group of Vikings led by Leif Eriksson set sail from Greenland. Heading west, they landed off the coast of what is now

Edmund was king of East Anglia in Britain when the Vikings invaded in 869. The king was captured and made the target of the Norsemen's archery practice. Christians revered Edmund as a martyr, and he was later canonized, or declared a saint.

Canada, where they established a settlement in Newfoundland.

The Vikings are often

IF IT'S THURSDAY, THANK THE VIKINGS

Sprinkled throughout the English language are many words the Vikings left behind to remind us to think of them every day. Or at least four days a week. The word *Tuesday* comes from the name of the Norse god of war, Tyr. Wednesday was named after Odin, or Woden, the Norsemen's supreme god. Thursday honors Thor, the god of thunder. Friday comes from "Frigga's day," for Frigga, the wife of Odin and the goddess of love and beauty.

A reconstruction of Viking houses in Sweden today.
Each house had one long room with a separate area for storing
grain or for keeping the farm animals in winter.

portrayed as nothing more than bloodthirsty savages, but that's partly because they were illiterate and couldn't write down their side of the story. It wasn't until the thirteenth century that Snorri Sturluson, the great poet from Iceland, wrote the story of the Norsemen and their exploits. Today we know that the Vikings founded a number of cities—Dublin, Limerick, Cork, and Waterford in Ireland alone—and that they were industrious traders. During the eleventh and twelfth centuries, the Vikings converted to Christianity and settled down to farming and other trades.

The end of the Viking Age is usually taken as the year 1066, when the Normans—the Norsemen who had settled in the north of France—streamed across the English Channel and overthrew the English king Harold I. The Norman leader took the throne as William I, or William the Conqueror. His descendants are still the kings and queens of England.

THE MUSLIMS IN SPAIN
A FUGITIVE PRINCE TAKES CHARGE

It was the year 750 according to the Christian calendar, and a young prince named Abd al-Rahman was running for his life. There was a revolution going on in the Middle East, a revolution whose effects would be felt as far away as Spain, and Abd al-Rahman was in the middle of it. His grandfather, who had ruled the Islamic empire of the Umayyads (oo-MY-ids), had just been killed. The Abbasids (ah-BAH-sids), a rival family, had overthrown the Umayyads, and they were determined to kill every heir to the Umayyad line, including Abd al-Rahman. Somehow the twenty-year-old prince had escaped, along with his thirteen-year-old brother. They found refuge with a group of Bedouin (Arab nomads) camped near the Euphrates River in northern Syria. Suddenly, from out of nowhere, horsemen thundered toward them, with the black banners of the Abbasids flying. The two fugitives leaped into the river. "Come back!" the attackers called. "We will not hurt you!" The younger boy—perhaps afraid he might not make it all the way across—decided to take them at their word. He swam back to shore and the attackers killed him. Abd al-Rahman kept swimming and escaped.

The young man fled through Palestine and across North Africa, alone and penniless, always looking over his shoulder in fear of his pursuers. Five years later, he reached Ceuta on the tip of North Africa, just across the Strait of Gibraltar from Spain, where uncles from his mother's side of the family took him in.

Before they were overthrown by the Abbasids, Abd al-Rahman's Umayyad ancestors had ruled the growing Islamic empire from their capital in Damascus, Syria, for more than a century. Muslims—believers in Islam—follow the teachings of the prophet Muhammad, who was born

Two hundred years after young Abd al-Rahman escaped his pursuers and founded a new dynasty in southern Spain, his descendant, Abd al-Rahman III, holds court.

in the city of Mecca on the Arabian peninsula around 570. Muhammad taught his followers to devote their lives to the praise and service of the one God, Allah. By the time the Prophet died in 632, the Arab people had

The Rock of Gibraltar, overlooking the point where Tariq and his men landed in the spring of 711. By the end of that summer, the Muslim conquerors held half of Spain.

converted from their pagan religion to Islam. They became a vibrant religious community as well as a political power, conquering territories all across North Africa. In time they would build one of the mightiest empires the world had ever seen.

In the year 711 Muslim Arabs invaded Spain. Their leader was Tariq ibn-Ziyad, who gave his name to the great rock that guards the western entrance to the Mediterranean Sea: Gibraltar (from the Arabic *Jabal Tariq*, "the mountain of Tariq"). Tariq and most of his men were Berbers, native peoples of North Africa who had converted to Islam and fought in the service of their Arab ruler. They expelled the Visigoths, a Germanic tribe that had ruled Spain since the 400s, and established Muslim rule there. The Muslims continued pushing north and got as far as central France, where they were halted in 732 by Charles Martel, grandfather of Charlemagne.

Some twenty years later, Abd al-Rahman arrived in Ceuta, gathered supporters, and crossed into Spain. Many cities opened their gates to welcome the heir to the great Umayyad family, but in some places Abd al-Rahman battled rival Arab chiefs. By 756 he had established himself as emir, or commander, of Muslim Spain, the land the Arabs called al-Andalus.

Abd al-Rahman built his capital in Córdoba. It wasn't long before the city became known as the "jewel of the world." While the rest of Europe was feeling its way through muddy thoroughfares in the dark, Córdoba had paved and lighted streets. It became a center of scholarship and poetry, and Europeans as well as Arabs flocked there. By the tenth century the city boasted the largest library in Europe, with some 400,000 volumes. The artisans of Córdoba were famous for their metalwork, leather, and textiles. Weavers made beautiful cloth of wool and of silk, a material new to Europe. From the Persians, Arab travelers had learned how to use silkworms to make silk, and they brought these methods to Spain. The secret of making paper, which the Arabs had learned from the Chinese, came to Europe through Muslim Spain.

Muslim rule in Spain was not only marked by its high level of culture, but also by a level of tolerance unusual for the times. Christians and Jews were generally respected for their abilities rather than punished for their religion, and many rose to positions of prominence. The Jews and Christians were seen as "people of the Book"—those who followed the

The splendid arches of the Great Mosque of Córdoba. Abd al-Rahman began construction of the mosque 785, building on a site where a Christian church had once stood and, before that, a Roman temple.

AN OLD DESSERT IN A NEW LIGHT

Rice pudding is a dessert you've probably eaten a hundred times. But you may not have realized that its main ingredients—rice and sugar—were unknown in Europe before the Arabs brought them to Spain. Our English words for rice and sugar, in fact, come from the Arabic language: "sugar" is *sukkar* in Arabic, and "rice" is *al-ruzz*.

The Arabs introduced many other crops to Europe, such as peaches, apricots, and oranges. They also brought irrigation methods that allowed crops to flourish in Spain's hot, dry climate.

If you like rice pudding, you may want to add an "al-Andalus" touch. First, make your favorite recipe, or simply buy ready-made pudding at the supermarket. Top with sliced peaches or bite-size pieces of dried apricots. (The Arabs also introduced a method for drying apricots and other fruits in the sun.) Then, to finish off your creation, you may want to sprinkle your pudding with rose water or orange blossom water (available in specialty food stores) for an authentic Middle Eastern flavor.

teachings of the Bible, as the Muslims followed the Koran, the holy book of Islam.

Abd al-Rahman ruled Muslim Spain until his death in 788. The dynasty he founded there would endure another two and a half centuries, until 1031, when the realm broke into a number of small territories ruled by independent Arab princes. The Arabs remained a powerful force in Spain until 1492, when they were finally expelled by the armies of the Catholic rulers Ferdinand and Isabella.

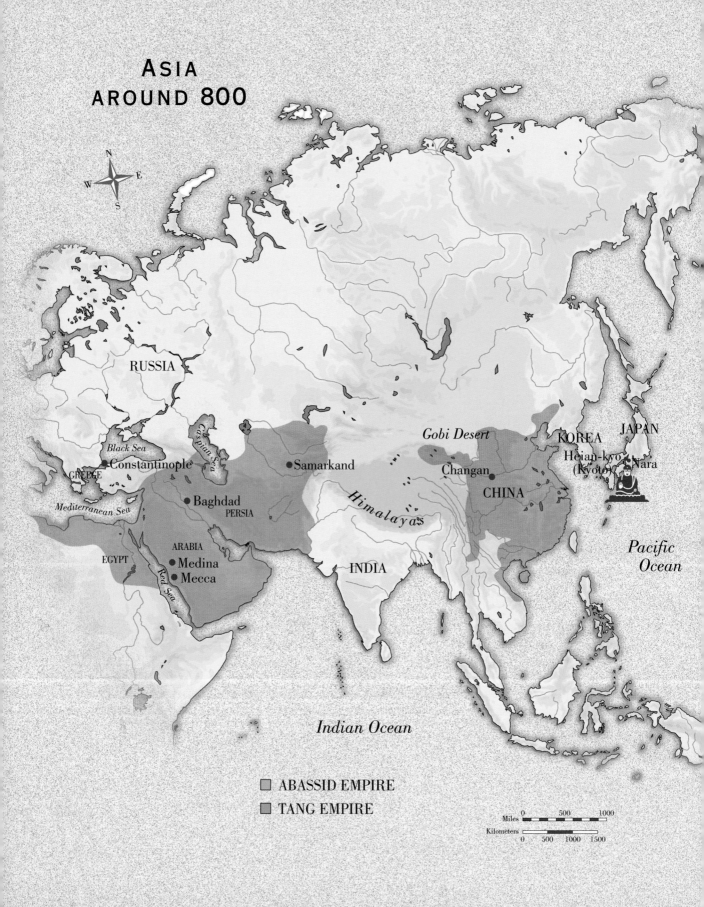

ASIA
AROUND 800

N W E S

RUSSIA

Black Sea
Constantinople
GREECE
Mediterranean Sea

Caspian Sea

Samarkand

Baghdad
PERSIA

ARABIA
Medina
Mecca

EGYPT

Red Sea

INDIA

Himalayas

Gobi Desert

Changan

CHINA

KOREA
Heian-kyo
(Kyoto)

JAPAN

Nara

*Pacific
Ocean*

Indian Ocean

ABASSID EMPIRE
TANG EMPIRE

Miles 0   500   1000

Kilometers 0   500   1000   1500

PART II

ASIA

In the year 800 two of the world's most important cities were in Asia: Baghdad, capital of the Islamic Empire in what is now Iraq, and Chan-gan, capital of the Tang dynasty in China. A third city, Constantinople, sat at the edge of Europe looking out to its lands in Asia. Constantinople was the capital of the Byzantine Empire, which around 800 ruled in Asia Minor as well as in parts of Europe. In these great cities people created treasures of art and poetry, and traded goods from all over the world. Knowledge, too, was a valued trading commodity: Arab scholars absorbed the writings of other cultures and added their own rich ideas, Japanese priests traveled to China to learn about Buddhism, and artists in India gave a Chinese monk the technology for making the first printed books in the world.

WHEN THEY RULED

The Abbasids
750–1258

Byzantium—The Isaurian Dynasty
717–820

Japan—The Heian Era
795–1185

China—The Tang Dynasty
618–907

THE ABBASIDS
HARUN AL-RASHID AND GLITTERING BAGHDAD

Harun al-Rashid (ha-ROON al-rah-SHEED) ruled one of the largest empires the world had ever seen. His lands stretched from the borders of India in the east to the middle of North Africa in the west. Harun was caliph (KAY-lif)—political and spiritual head—of the Abbasid Empire. The Abbasids were the Muslim dynasty that had overthrown the Umayyads in 750 and sent Abd al-Rahman fleeing to Spain. The fifth caliph of the Abbasids, Harun ruled from 786 to 809.

He knew of Charlemagne, although the two never met. In about 800 Charlemagne sent his ambassadors to Harun's court. Harun sent them back with gifts: silks and brocades, expensive perfumes, an elaborate water clock, and an elephant. It was said that, when the elephant died during one of Charlemagne's campaigns, the emperor had the tusks made into chess pieces.

Harun's capital city, Baghdad, had been built by his grandfather al-Mansur, "the Victorious." By Harun's time Baghdad was "a city with no equal in the world," as an eleventh-century Arab historian put it. It was the largest city outside China, with a population that may have reached a half million.

Baghdad was a center of learning, art, and poetry, as well as an important hub of trade. Ships from as far away as China and Africa docked along its wharves. If you could have taken a stroll through the bazaars of Baghdad in 800, you would have found silk and porcelain from China; panthers and coconuts from India; rubies, fine carpets, and slaves from central Asia; honey, furs, and more slaves from Scandinavia and Russia; ivory, gold, and slaves from Africa; rice and linen from Egypt; and pearls and horses from Arabia. You would have found the world in Baghdad.

Harun's court was renowned for its luxury. The caliph apparently had

Harun al-Rashid receives ambassadors from Charlemagne. Harun became a romantic figure to Western audiences through the stories of The 1001 Nights. *In these stories, introduced to Europeans in the early 1700s, Harun goes about the streets of Baghdad in disguise, eavesdropping on the lives of ordinary people and ensuring that their tales have a happy ending.*

This medieval miniature, painted around 1250, shows shops in a bazaar very much like one you might have seen in Baghdad in the year 800. In the archway at the far left is the jeweler; then the herbalist, who sells spices and herbs; the butcher; and the baker.

a special liking for jewels. When he acquired an enormous ruby that had been owned by several kings of Persia, he had his name inscribed on it. A medieval historian reported that, "if [the ruby] were put in the night-time in a dark room it would shine like a lamp." Harun's wife, Zubaydah, also fancied jewels and started a fashion by wearing them on her shoes. The royal table, too, glittered with goblets of gold and silver encrusted with precious stones.

The people of Baghdad enjoyed many luxuries, especially in the way of food. From farms south of the city came delicious fruits and vegetables. From central Asia came lemons, apricots, figs, grapes, pomegranates, and watermelons. The watermelons were placed in lead molds and packed in ice so that they would be fresh upon arrival.

Baghdad was a good place to live for another reason: it was the place to be for state-of-the-art health care. Harun himself is credited with establishing the first real hospital in the Islamic world. Like many of today's teaching hospitals, it was a place where the sick were treated and doctors were educated at the same time.

Harun hired a Christian doctor named Bakhtishu for his hospital. Bakhtishu had practiced at a famous hospital in Persia. He and his colleagues had studied the medical texts of the Persians and the Indians, who in turn had learned much from the writings of ancient Greek physicians.

One of the most important physicians to practice in Baghdad was al-Razi, who lived from 864 to 930. He wrote more than one hundred books, including a chemistry text that remained the major authority on the subject until the fourteenth century. Al-Razi's most important work,

Literature, too, reached new heights in Abbasid times. The Maqamat of al-Hariri are a collection of entertaining stories told in beautiful, flowery language. The book became a model for elegant Arabic and is still read today. On this page from a thirteenth-century manuscript, Abu Zayd, the witty, eloquent rascal who appears in all the stories, comes upon two merchants climbing onto their camels.

A SLAVE REBELLION THREATENS THE ABBASIDS

Slavery was a fact of life in the medieval world. The Vikings and the Franks took their defeated enemies as slaves and also bought slaves from traders. The Abbasids got their slaves from Europe, central Asia, and Africa. Some slaves were treated well and rose to important positions. Harun al-Rashid's mother was a slave who came to wield a great deal of power. But many slaves faced lives of misery and hardship.

In the ninth century East African slaves were brought to what is now southern Iraq to work in salt mines and on plantations. The conditions there were terrible, and in 869 the slaves revolted. *Zanj* is the Arabic word for "black African," and so the uprising was called the Zanj Rebellion. The former slaves set up their own state, and they even tried to turn the tables and enslave their former masters. They sacked the city of Basra and controlled much of southern Iraq for several years. Southern Iraq is covered with salt marshes and has long been a favorite refuge for anyone wishing to escape the law. The rebels established their city in the marshes, where it was difficult for Abbasid troops to reach them. It was not until 883 that the Abbasids regained control of the area.

al-Hawi, is an encyclopedia of medical knowledge. It was translated into Latin in 1279 and continuously reprinted until 1542. Al-Razi's works provided the foundation for Western medical training for many centuries.

In other areas of learning, the Arabs took the same approach they took in medicine: they sought out texts written by the authorities—the ancient Greeks, the Persians, the Indians, the Chinese—and translated them

*A slave market in Baghdad. At the top, a merchant weighs
coins a buyer has offered. Below, black African slaves
await their fate, as would-be buyers approach them.*

into Arabic. They learned all they could from these works, and then
they added their own ideas.

The Abbasid rulers were great patrons of learning. Harun collected and
studied Greek manuscripts on science and philosophy and hired scholars
to translate them into Arabic. Later, the caliph al-Ma'mun, who ruled from
813 to 833, founded one of the world's most important centers of learning,

Bayt al-Hikma, or the "House of Wisdom" in Baghdad. The institution included an observatory from which astronomers could record the movements of celestial bodies, determine when the equinoxes would fall,

Abbasid ladies and gentlemen pampered themselves with elaborate baths taken in specially designed, luxuriously decorated rooms. In this miniature the Caliph Harun al-Rashid is scrubbed and shaved, while some attendants bring buckets of water and others hang the towels to dry.

IN THE YEAR OF THE HEGIRA

The Christian calendar, based on the date of Christ's birth, was hardly appropriate for Muslims. They needed their own calendar to mark time. The event they took for the beginning of their era was the year the prophet Muhammad moved from Mecca, the city where he was born, to Medina. In Mecca Muhammad and his followers were being persecuted for their beliefs, and a plan had been hatched to murder the Prophet. The people of Medina, though, recognized Muhammad's leadership skills and invited him to their city, hoping he might help resolve disputes there. The Prophet's escape to Medina—called the Hegira, from the Arabic *hijrah*, or "flight"— was important in the history of Islam because it marked the time when Muhammad became a political leader as well as a religious leader. The date falls in the year 622 in the Christian calendar. Dates in the Islamic calendar are written in English with the notation a.h. (*anno Hegirae*, Latin for "in the year of the Hegira").

The Islamic calendar is lunar—based on the phases of the moon— and each of its twelve months begins when the first sliver of the new moon appears. The lunar year has 354 days. It is 11 days shorter than a year in the calendar used in the West, which is based on the earth's movement around the sun. This shorter year means that the months of the Islamic calendar move up through the seasons 11 days every year. Unlike holidays in the West, Islamic feasts and holy days fall at different times and in different seasons each year.

and calculate the length of the solar year, all with remarkable precision. The movement of the earth was of special importance to Muslims, who are supposed to pray five times a day. The hours of prayer vary according to the sun's position in the sky. Arab mathematicians used advanced mathematics

THE VERY MODEL OF A NINTH-CENTURY GENTLEMAN

Just as people today consult books on fashion and manners, people in the ninth century looked for guidance, too. One Abbasid writer offered the following advice to the would-be gentleman: refrain from joking; choose your friends carefully; never stray from truthfulness; be scrupulous in keeping promises and secrets; wear clothes that are not patched or dirty; while eating, take small mouthfuls, chew slowly, don't talk, and don't lick your fingers; avoid garlic and onions; and don't use a toothpick in public places.

and a sophisticated understanding of the earth's rotation to calculate precisely the times for prayer. We have many words in English borrowed from Arabic to remind us of Arab contributions in mathematics and astronomy: among them, algebra, algorithm, cipher, zero, zenith, and the names of many stars.

Technology can have a profound effect on the way people live. Computers have made dramatic changes in our lives. In Harun's time the new idea was paper. The Chinese knew how to make paper from flax, linen, or hemp rags, but they would not share their technology. Their secret got out, however, in the seventh century, and paper turned up in India. Then, in 751, Muslim armies fighting in Samarkand, in central Asia, learned the secret from Chinese war prisoners. Paper was soon being produced in Baghdad.

By the tenth century there were paper mills all across the Arab world. Before that, books had been written on parchment or papyrus, both of which were much more expensive than paper. The widespread production of paper meant that many more people could have books. One of the best-known writers of Harun's time, al-Jahiz (al-JA-hiz), wrote these words about books:

> I can think of no item so new, born so recently, yet modest in price and easily obtained, that brings together so much excellent advice, so much rare knowledge, so many works by great minds...so much information about ancient times, distant lands, popular sayings, and ruined empires, as a book.
>
> A book is a companion...of whom you never tire.

As with all new technologies, some people had mixed feelings about books and the possibilities for learning they brought. Stories grew up illustrating the dangers of too much learning. There is a legend about al-Jahiz himself: it is said that he met his death by being smothered under an avalanche of books!

THE BYZANTINES
INSULTS FOR THE EMPERORS

As a young man, Harun al-Rashid commanded the Muslim armies against the Byzantine Empire. In 782 his forces threatened Constantinople. The infamous Irene, who would later have her son blinded and take the throne, was ruling at that time in her young son's name. Irene was forced to accept a humiliating peace, agreeing to pay Harun large sums in tribute. By 802 Irene had been overthrown by Nicephorus I. The new Byzantine emperor attempted to cancel the treaty she had made. Not only did he refuse to pay the tribute, he also wrote demanding a refund of what had already been paid. Needless to say, Harun was furious. He dashed off his reply on the back of the emperor's letter:

> In the name of God, the merciful, the compassionate. From Harun, the commander of the believers, to Nicephorus, the dog of a Roman…. I have read thy letter, O son of an infidel mother. As for the answer it shall be for thine eye to see, not for thine ear to hear. Salam [Goodbye].

The infamous empress Irene

Wealthy Byzantine women such as these would have spent much of their lives at home, shielded from the gaze of men outside the family. When they were allowed to venture out—for religious celebrations or to attend public baths reserved for women—they would have worn veils.

Harun then sent out his armies, ravaging Asia Minor and capturing some important Byzantine cities. He demanded that Nicephorus pay both the tribute and an even more insulting tax on the emperor himself and each member of his household. This moment marked the peak of Abbasid power. By the tenth century, their empire had broken up. (The Abbasid dynasty itself would end in the thirteenth century when Baghdad was sacked by the Mongols, warriors from central Asia.)

The Byzantines, on the other hand, enjoyed renewed splendor and power under the reign of Emperor Basil I in the late ninth century. Under Basil, the Byzantine army was strengthened, new laws protected the poor, and art and architecture flourished. Two centuries later, however, attacks by Arab and Norman invaders weakened the Byzantine Empire. In the 1200s the empire was split into three parts. In 1453, after a brave and desperate defense, the Byzantine capital at Constantinople fell to the Muslims of the Ottoman Empire, who renamed the great city Istanbul.

THE JAPANESE
A STATUE COMES TO LIFE

In 752 an important ceremony was taking place in the Japanese capital of Nara, one that brought ten thousand priests and other dignitaries from the far reaches of Japan, China, and India. A giant statue of the Buddha was being consecrated. The statue was symbolically brought to life as a priest from India painted pupils into its eyes.

The Japanese emperor had built the statue in hopes of appeasing the gods, who had allowed a terrible smallpox epidemic to sweep through the land. It took more than ten years to build the fifty-two-foot-high Buddha, which contained more than a million pounds of copper, tin, and lead. Five hundred pounds of gold covered the awe-inspiring image.

Buddhism had come to Japan from China, by way of Korea, in the sixth century A.D. The religion had been founded in India around 500 B.C. by a prince named Siddhartha Gautama, later called the Buddha, or "the enlightened one." Siddhartha gave up his riches and set out as a poor wanderer to find the meaning of life. Through his meditations he came to believe that life is an illusion and that, when one realizes this, all worldly desires vanish. Desire, the Buddha taught, is the cause of suffering. By getting rid of desire, a person can escape suffering and reach a state of nirvana, or total peace.

By the time Buddhism came to Japan, the Japanese people already had a religion: Shinto, or "the way of the gods." Shinto is a simple faith, with no scriptures or moral directives. Instead it teaches a joyful reverence for all of nature. Shinto gods are called *kami*. A *kami* might be the spirit of a long-departed ancestor, or it might be a spirit living in a mountain, a brook, or a beautiful butterfly. The most important of the *kami* was Amaterasu,

The statue of the Great Buddha at Nara still stands today.

the sun goddess. Around the third century, a clan who worshipped Amaterasu came to power, and its leader declared that he was the goddess's son. After that, up until modern times, all of Japan's emperors claimed to be descended from Amaterasu.

When Buddhism swept across Japan, the emperors—who based their authority on their connection to Amaterasu—had to find a way for the two religions to coexist. So while the giant statue of the Buddha was being built at Nara, an important Buddhist priest was sent to the shrine of Amaterasu. He prayed there for seven days and seven nights. Finally the goddess herself spoke. In a clear, melodious voice, Amaterasu recited a poem welcoming the great Buddha as she would a "boat at a crossing or a torch in the darkness."

By the end of the 700s, the Buddhist priests in Nara had become very powerful—too powerful for the emperor's taste. He thought it was time for a change. He ordered a new capital to be built thirty miles north of Nara and moved the government there in 794. The city was called Heian-kyo, "the Capital of Peace and Tranquility." Later it became known simply as Kyoto, "the capital."

In the court at Kyoto, the emperor performed Shinto rituals and ceremonies to ensure Japan's good fortune. Meanwhile, elegantly dressed court nobles lived in luxury, playing music, writing

A woodblock print from the nineteenth century illustrates an episode from the Japanese creation myth. Amaterasu, the sun goddess, is hiding in a cave because her brother has insulted her. To entice her out of the cave, other gods perform a raucous dance. Amaterasu, hearing the laughter and merriment, cannot contain her curiosity. She emerges from the cave and brings light back into the world.

A group of nobles entertain themselves by practicing the art of calligraphy.

poetry, and practicing the art of calligraphy, or graceful writing with brush and ink. All their arts reflected Japan's unique blend of faiths, combining the Shinto appreciation of nature with Buddhism's search for religious enlightenment.

To this day, Shinto and Buddhism exist side by side in Japan. A family may hold a Shinto wedding but follow Buddhist traditions for a funeral. The Japanese honor the *kami* by visiting Shinto shrines and enjoying Shinto festivals. They also pray at Buddhist temples and try to lead a good life by following Buddhism's moral guidelines. Even in the popular sport of sumo wrestling, the two faiths have their place: Salt—used in Shinto rituals to banish death and disease—is still sprinkled by the wrestlers to purify the sumo-wrestling ring. But the sport owes its emphasis on discipline of mind and body to Buddhism.

THE CHINESE
LONG-LASTING PEACE AND EVERLASTING SORROW

China in the eighth and ninth centuries—at the height of the Tang dynasty—was one of the most advanced societies in the world. It was, in fact, a model the rest of the world was eager to copy. The Japanese regularly sent scholars, priests, and diplomats to the Tang capital, Changan. The Japanese found Changan, whose name means "long-lasting peace," so beautiful that they copied its design for their own capital at Nara. The Japanese even borrowed the Chinese writing system, which they later adapted to suit their needs.

Muslims, too, took much from Chinese culture. The prophet Muhammad had said, "Seek knowledge, even if it takes you to China," and many Muslims followed his advice. Some traveled to China for knowledge, while others went in search of the beautiful luxury items China was famous for: gorgeous silks and delicate porcelain pottery. The first Arab ship docked at a Chinese port during the time of Harun al-Rashid, in about 787, and for the next five centuries, the Arabs controlled trade between China and Europe.

What did travelers find when they reached the famous Chinese capital? Changan was a marvel, with a million inhabitants living within its three-story-high brick walls and another million in the surrounding suburbs. The city itself was a rectangle six miles by five miles, with streets laid out in a perfect grid, to reflect the harmonious proportions of paradise. Once inside the main gate, visitors could follow an avenue five hundred feet wide to the imperial palace. The city was cosmopolitan—people from all over the world thronged its busy streets.

In Tang China the wealthy lived in comfort and luxury. Their homes, outfitted with bathrooms and water fountains, were kept comfortable by mechanical fans that circulated ice-cooled breezes in summer and warm

A view, painted in the 1700s, of the emperor's palace in Tang China. The emperor sits in the top room of the palace while the courtiers and servants go about their work below.

air from a charcoal brazier in winter. Princes and princesses mounted on the finest horses money could buy played polo, a sport imported from Persia. Women enjoyed a great deal of freedom. Besides competing with men on the polo field, they wrote poetry and wielded power in politics. Both noblemen and noblewomen wore jewelry of gold and silver and

Elegant women of the Tang court enjoy a feast serenaded by musicians. The guests sip wine from porcelain bowls while a little dog sleeps under the table.

doted on their favorite pets, lapdogs brought from central Asia. The Chinese also bred their own version of these "just-for-looks" pets—small, long-coated dogs known today as Pekingese.

Despite its wealth and advances, though, all was not peaceful in Tang China. From 755 to 763 a rebellion, with a cast of characters that included a beautiful woman and an enormously fat military governor, shook the dynasty to its very foundations. Some years earlier, the emperor Xuan-cang (SHOO-an-sahng) had begun appointing non-Chinese soldiers as governors of the crucial frontier provinces. He thought that, since these men had no ties to China's ruling classes, they would have no political ambitions. He was quite wrong. One foreign governor who rose to prominence was An Lu-shan, a fat, witty Turk who had been put in charge of the province in the extreme northeast. His success brought him to the attention of the emperor and the emperor's favorite, a woman named Yang Kui-fei (yong kway-fay).

Yang Kui-fei is a famous figure in Chinese history, a woman of legendary beauty who used her charms to gain power for herself and her friends. When she took a fancy to An Lu-shan, she adopted him as her son. But many of those in power resented An Lu-shan's special place and tried to undermine him.

Meanwhile, the prime minister died, and An Lu-shan and one of Yang Kui-fei's cousins became embroiled in a bitter struggle to succeed him. The cousin won and became prime minister. An Lu-shan responded by leading a series of bloody battles against him, destroying cities and even attacking the capital. The emperor and Yang Kui-fei were forced to flee Changan, and the country was plunged into civil war.

The emperor's guards blamed the beautiful woman for the country's troubles and demanded her life as well as the life of her cousin, the prime minister. With unspeakable sadness the emperor ordered the execution of his beloved. Yang Kui-fei was strangled and her body thrown into a ditch. The story lives on in a famous poem called "The Song of Everlasting Sorrow," by the Tang poet Po Chu-i (poe choo-EE).

Xuan-cang, who had once ruled so wisely that he was known as "Brilliant Emperor," came to a sad and bitter end. As violence continued to rock the country, he was forced to renounce the throne in favor of his son. In 757 An Lu-shan was assassinated, but it was not until 763 that the rebellion was finally put down.

The civil war planted lasting fears in the hearts of China's citizens. Their country had been ravaged. Even the magnificent capital had been looted and burned. The frontiers were no longer secure. The central government no longer had the authority it once did. Although the Tang dynasty held on to power for another 140 years, its empire was never quite the same. In 907 a final bloody rebellion devastated Changan. The capital's days of glory were over, and the Tang dynasty was finished.

THE FIRST PRINTED BOOK

If you look at Chinese writing, you'll see what appears to be a lot of small, separate blocks marching up and down the page. The blocks are symbols, or characters. The Chinese use these characters instead of letters to form words.

Some Chinese characters are simple pictures that look something like the word they represent. The character for *tree*, for example, looks like a tree trunk with branches sticking out. Other, more complicated characters are made by combining two or more parts, or elements. One element may help identify the word, while another tells how it is pronounced. Sometimes the elements are combinations of simple characters. *Forest*, for example, is a combination of three tree characters, one on top of the other. The word *bright* is made by joining together the characters for *sun* and *moon*.

Tang China was a natural place to produce the world's first printed books. All the necessary ingredients were there. The Chinese loved the look of their written characters, and writing beautifully—calligraphy—was considered a high art. Students spent years mastering calligraphy, learning how to hold the brush just right and how to make the strokes for each character in just the right order and the right size. The Chinese also had plenty of paper—they had invented it at least as early as A.D. 110—and a long history of rich literature. And a Chinese character fits nicely onto a square block, which was the basic tool of the first printers.

Printing came to China by way of an idea borrowed from India. A Chinese monk visiting India around 670 noticed that people there were taking wooden blocks carved with pictures of the Buddha, dipping them in ink, and pressing them onto silk or paper to make a picture. This was a revolutionary new technology, and the Chinese monk brought it home. The Chinese were soon carving not pictures but characters into blocks, dipping the blocks in ink, and pressing the inked blocks onto paper or cloth to make books.

By the year 800 books were being printed not only in China but also in

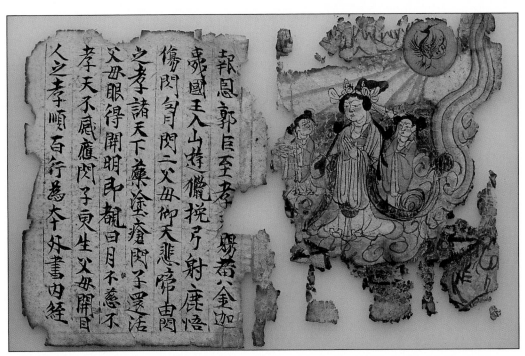

Before printing was invented, every character in a book had to be penned with painstaking care by a master who had spent years studying the art of calligraphy. This fragment of a Tang dynasty manuscript was found in a temple in western China. The character at the top of the far left column means "man."

Korea and Japan, regions that borrowed many ideas from the Chinese. The oldest printed book that survives today dates from 868. Discovered in a cave in northwest China in 1907, the book is a copy of a Buddhist text called the Diamond Sutra. It is made of individual sheets glued to a backing to form a scroll about seventeen feet long by ten inches wide. By the year 1000 modern-style books with pages had replaced scrolls. Another 450 years would pass before the German inventor Johannes Gutenberg would come up with some new ideas for movable type, build a printing press, and print the first books in the West.

AFRICA AROUND 800

Mediterranean Sea

Kairouan

Baghdad

Sahara Desert

Nile River

Mecca

Red Sea

Kumbi Salih

Niger River

Jenné-jeno

Atlantic Ocean

N
W E
S

Indian Ocean

■ EMPIRE OF GHANA
■ AGHLABID EMPIRE

Miles 0 200 500

Kilometers 0 300 600 900

PART III

AFRICA

Africa is vast and varied. The Sahara Desert covers the top third of the continent, and grasslands, thick forests, mountains, and more deserts cover the rest. African civilization is very old, and the African continent was likely the home of the first humans. Many different kinds of societies have made their homes in Africa: traders, farmers, nomads, and city folk.

We do not know very much about the details of life in Africa around 800. We can't read the stories the peoples told about themselves or their heroes, because they left no written records. They lived in prehistoric societies. "Prehistoric" does not have to mean very long ago; the word simply means before *written* history. Instead of writing, African societies had a strong oral tradition. They passed important information from generation to generation in songs and stories. Another source for information is the accounts written by travelers from other parts of the world.

WHEN THEY RULED
North Africa: The Aghlabids
800–909

The Kingdom of Ghana
c. 300–1100

NORTH AFRICA
A TOUR OF A GREAT MOSQUE

One of the landmarks that you might see on your trip to North Africa in 800 is the Great Mosque of Kairouan (ker-WAHN), in modern-day Tunisia. The town of Kairouan was founded in 670 by Arab conquerors. At first it served as a camp from which Arab armies launched their raids across North Africa, conquering vast territories and converting the population to Islam. By 800 an Arab dynasty called the Aghlabids ruled about a third of North Africa. They chose Kairouan for their capital. The city became a lively place, a crossroads for trade and commerce and a center of Islamic culture.

The Great Mosque of Kairouan was not always great. It started out as a modest building and over the years was enlarged several times. The center of community and religious life for Muslims, mosques are

The Great Mosque of Kairouan seen from the air. The tower in the center of the foreground is the minaret. The muezzin—a man with a beautiful voice—climbs the stairs to the top of the minaret five times every day to call people to prayer. The prayer hall is in the far end of the mosque, under the domes.

A man guides his loaded donkey through a narrow street in Kairouan, a scene you might have witnessed in the year 800.

very much the same across the Islamic world. Let's imagine what it would have been like to take a tour through Kairouan and the Great Mosque around the year 800:

Come along through the bustling streets of Kairouan. Watch out for the horses and the donkey carts! Traders just arriving from a long journey lead their camels past us, laden with goods from the African kingdoms to the south. People are dressed in long robes, many of them in white or somber

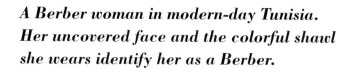

A Berber woman in modern-day Tunisia. Her uncovered face and the colorful shawl she wears identify her as a Berber.

gray. We also see some Berber tribespeople wearing bright colors, the men covering their faces with blue cloths. The streets are narrow, as are most city streets in this part of the world, so that the buildings can provide shade from the blazing sun.

As we walk toward the mosque, we hear a clear, powerful voice calling out over the noise of the crowd. It is the muezzin (moo-EH-zen), telling people to come to prayers. It is Friday, the day Muslims worship together, and people pour into the streets on their way to the mosque. Carried along by the crowd, we approach a building with tall, plain walls. Mosques are often plain on the outside, giving no clue to their interiors.

We let ourselves be pulled in with the crowd through one of the doors to the mosque. Inside, sunlight streams across a large open courtyard. We must take off our shoes, because this is holy ground. At a fountain worshipers stop to wash their faces, hands, and feet in preparation for prayer. Then the crowd moves toward the far

The prayer hall of the Great Mosque of Kairouan.

end of the courtyard. Rows of columns stretch out on both sides and in front of us. Passing through a wide archway between the rows of columns, we pause a moment to let our eyes adjust to the shadows in this covered area, the prayer hall. We are standing in a forest of beautiful columns, each with an intricately carved top on which rest arches holding up the ceiling that seems to float above our heads.

Worshipers are settling down on the carpets that cover the stone floor. With their legs folded under them, they touch their heads to the ground, then sit up straight and wait for prayers to begin. They are sitting in rows, all facing the wall at the front. Set into that wall is a niche, or recess, decorated with carved marble and shiny tiles brought specially from Baghdad for this important mosque. Every mosque has a niche, called a mihrab. It may not always be so elegantly decorated as the one in Kairouan, but it is always positioned to mark the direction of Mecca. Muslims are supposed to face Mecca, the holiest city of Islam, when they pray. We watch as the imam, the man who leads the prayer service, climbs the steps of the intricately carved wooden pulpit to the right of the mihrab. Worship has begun. And as we hear the chanting of ancient scriptures, we know that all across the world—in grand mosques like this and in many humbler places— Muslims are turning their faces toward Mecca in prayer.

WEST AFRICA
THE GOLDEN EMPIRE OF GHANA

The eighth-century Arab traders who first visited and wrote about West Africa described the empire of Ghana as a "land of gold." The ancient empire of Ghana was situated within the present-day countries of Mali and Mauritania. It was a powerful and wealthy state that reached its height of power between the years 400 and 800.

Much of what we know about the early history of West Africa comes from the writings of the Arab scholar al-Bakri, who lived around the year 1000. Al-Bakri based his information on reports of traders and other travelers to Ghana. The empire was so rich, he wrote, that even the dogs had golden collars. He went on to describe the capital, Kumbi Salih: it had two districts, a Muslim area where wealthy Arab traders lived, and a royal compound, where the *ghana*, or warlord, and his family and retainers lived.

The riches of Ghana came mainly from its gold and salt. We know that West Africans traded gold with the Roman Empire as far back as the fourth century, and maybe earlier. Later, West African gold found its way to North Africa, the Middle East, India, and the Far East. Gold became the standard currency in the Islamic empires of North Africa, and in the eighth century mints for making gold coins were built in the city of Kairouan and in Egypt.

Of course, to get to these places, the gold and other costly goods had to be carried across the Sahara Desert. The journey was treacherous. Travelers

*A caravan at rest in Kabylia, a region in North Africa that
is part of Algeria today. Wealthy travelers to Ghana would have
enjoyed the relative comfort of a palanquin, the wide covered seat
mounted on the camel. The Berbers who live in this area today, called
Kabyles, still wear the wide straw hats we see in this painting.*

could become disoriented and lose their way in a sandstorm or miss a water
hole and die of thirst. The remains of one ill-fated caravan that set out in the
twelfth century were discovered recently. Amid the skeletons of the camels

A quiet street scene in Djenné, a city in modern-day Mali, which sits on the edge of the Sahara Desert. About two miles from Djenné is the site of its ancient predecessor, Jenné-jeno, an important stop along the trade routes that connected West Africa with East Africa and with Islamic North Africa. Jenné-jeno flourished from about 450 until 1100, growing rich from trade in gold, copper, salt, and other goods.

and the unfortunate travelers was the precious cargo: two thousand brass bars weighing nearly a ton.

Ghana also controlled the West African trade in salt. Since ancient times salt has been highly prized. It not only adds flavor to food but also is excellent for preserving meats and other perishable foods, so it was especially valued in the days before refrigeration. West African rulers kept the locations of their salt mines secret and heavily guarded. They

A GOLDEN COURT

Around the year 1000 the Arab historian al-Bakri wrote detailed descriptions of the West African kingdoms, including the empire of Ghana. Al-Bakri lived in Córdoba, the city that Abd al-Rahman had made the capital of Muslim Spain and the "jewel of the world." Apparently, the historian was very comfortable in the city. Although his accounts are considered one of the most valuable sources of information on eleventh-century West Africa, he never actually left Córdoba to visit the lands he described. Instead al-Bakri based his accounts on reports by and interviews with traders and explorers who did cross the Sahara.

The empire of Ghana was at its height of wealth and grandeur during the years of al-Bakri's investigations. The ruler at the time was Tunka Menin. Al-Bakri provided this description of the golden splendors of Tunka's court.

> When [the king] gives audience to his people, to listen to their complaints and set them to rights, he sits in a pavilion around which stand his horses caparisoned [covered] in cloth of gold; behind him stand ten pages holding shields and gold-mounted swords; and on his right hand are the sons of the princes of his empire, splendidly clad [dressed] and with gold plaited into their hair. The governor of the city is seated on the ground in front of the king, and all around him are his viziers [important officers] in the same position. The gate of the chamber is guarded by dogs of an excellent breed, who never leave the king's seat; they wear collars of gold and silver.

traded salt for slaves, ivory, spices, and foods from the southern grasslands and forests. In the Middle Ages salt was so precious that some people would even exchange gold for an equal weight of salt.

In 1076 Muslim Berbers from North Africa invaded the empire of Ghana and captured its capital. Contact with Arab traders over the centuries had already brought Islam to Ghana, and the Berber invasion helped to further spread the faith. By the twelfth century Ghana's rulers had converted to Islam. They had also regained their independence. Within another hundred years, though, invasions by rival empires badly weakened Ghana. The remains of the empire were swallowed up by the ancient kingdom of Mali. According to legend, the descendants of the vanished empire of Ghana migrated south, to find new homes in the present-day nation of Ghana.

The Great Mosque at Djenné is the largest mud mosque in the world. Besides being a place of worship, the mosque unites the community in the ongoing project of replastering. Every spring the town holds a festival in which the masons of Djenné compete to replaster the walls of the mosque. These craftsmen, who have passed down the art of building with mud from generation to generation, pride themselves on their skills. When they go to work on the mosque, they scramble up the poles that protrude from the walls, using them as ladders. Mud buildings must be replastered from time to time or their walls will melt during the rainy season.

Pacific
Ocean

Atlantic
Ocean

N
W   E
S

Cahokia

Snaketown

Sonoran
Desert

Mississippi River

Chichén Itzá
Palenque   YUCATÁN
Tikal   PENINSULA
CANCUÉN   Copán

THE AMERICAS
AROUND 800

☐ THE MISSISSIPPIANS
☐ HOHOKAM
☐ MAYA

Miles   0   500   1000   1500

Kilometers 0   1000   2000

PART IV

THE AMERICAS

If you were strapped into your time machine, hurtling back to the year 800, you would see some remarkable sights as you passed over the Americas. In North America, near the Mississippi River, a gigantic earthen pyramid is rising. In the Southwest great dams and miles and miles of canals wind along the desert floor. In Mesoamerica, the narrow strip of land that connects North and South America, magnificent stone temples poke out above the green of the rain forest.

Many cultures were flourishing in the Americas around 800. Let's visit a few of them.

WHEN THEY RULED
The Mississippian Culture
c. 800–1500

The Hohokam Culture
c. 300–1350

The Maya—Classic Period
c. 250–900

THE MISSISSIPPIANS
CAHOKIA, MIGHTY CITY OF MOUNDS

Around 800 a town was taking shape near the banks of the Mississippi River, not far from where Saint Louis stands today. Its name was Cahokia (kah-HO-kee-ah), and it was to become the largest and most important settlement of the Mississippians. The Mississippians were the ancient people who lived in the large region of North America that is drained by the Mississippi River. This area stretches all the way from the Great Plains in the west to the Appalachian Mountains in the east. The civilization of these early North Americans appeared in the early ninth century A.D.

The town of Cahokia reached its peak between 900 and 1200, when about 16,000 people lived there. What was unusual about Cahokia was its many mounds—small hills with flat tops—and earthen pyramids. One pyramid towered over all the others. It was built with steps leading up to a huge, flat platform at the top. Archaeologists have dubbed this pyramid Monks Mound. It covered 14 acres—nearly the size of fourteen football fields. Scattered around the great pyramid were many smaller pyramids and mounds, along with huts where people lived, workshops, and gardens. The entire settlement was surrounded by a high fence made of poles placed tightly one after the other. Outside the protective fence were additional homes as well as fields for growing food.

Archaeologists believe that Monks Mound was built in stages over the course of several hundred years, from around 800 to 1200. At first glance, you might think that the pyramid is not much more than a pile of dirt. But for the dirt to stay put for a thousand years, as it has, a well-engineered structure had to be in place underneath. The architects of Cahokia designed the pyramid with a core of tightly packed earth. This core supported layers

One of the mounds at Cahokia as it looks today, its lines still neat and symmetrical, testimony to the engineering skills of its builders. Flat-topped mounds like this one supported important buildings and homes of the elite. Other mounds were used for burials.

of softer dirt that were gradually built up around it. Workers alternated layers of sand and clay to allow rainfall to drain through the earth and to prevent erosion. The entire structure was built in what must have been a painstakingly slow way—basketful by basketful of dirt.

Perhaps not unlike Christian churches, with their tall steeples that dominate the landscape and are meant to inspire people with thoughts of God, Monks Mound stood out as a sacred place. But what were the other mounds and pyramids used for? Archaeologists think that public buildings were constructed on some and homes for important people on others. Some mounds were set aside for the dead. The Mississippians at Cahokia had an unusual burial practice. When someone died, the body was laid out and placed on top of a pyramid, where it was exposed to the elements. After the flesh decayed, the bones were covered over with earth.

The Mississippians lived a sophisticated life compared to the ways of the people before them. One of the things that set Mississippian culture apart was that the people had a steady, dependable source of food. Although maize, or corn, had been cultivated by North Americans for close to two thousand years, it had long been just one crop of many. Sometime between 800 and 1000, however, the Mississippians cultivated a stronger kind of corn that could better survive disease and cold weather. Some archaeologists think that this strain of corn was brought from Mexico by traders. Wherever it came from, the corn was dependable enough for it to become the staple—the main food—of the Mississippians. With food in plentiful supply, the population grew.

More people eventually meant that more farmland was needed. Archaeologists believe that the Mississippians were a warlike people, attacking neighboring lands to increase their territory. To make war, the Mississippians used an invention relatively new to North America: the bow and arrow. For thousands of years, until 600, when the bow and arrow appeared, North Americans had used spears with stone points for weapons. But when someone came up with the idea of the bow and arrow, its advantages became obvious. A flint-tipped arrow propelled by a bow could travel three times as far as a spear and could be aimed with much greater accuracy.

No one is certain what happened to the people of Cahokia. By 1400, however, their city of mounds and pyramids had been abandoned. The people probably moved away little by little over a period of time and established new communities elsewhere.

Thatch and pole huts such as this modern-day model were home to the people of Cahokia.

THE HOHOKAM
MAKING THE DESERT BLOOM

The Hohokam (ho-ho-KAHM) lived in the Sonoran Desert in what is today Arizona. At first they were nomads, moving from place to place in search of food. Around 600 they became skilled farmers, which allowed them to settle down and live in villages. But farming was a challenge in the desert Southwest, where rainfall averaged only seven to ten inches a year. If they were going to succeed at farming, the people had to learn to harness the available water. By trial and error, it seems, they learned to build canals and irrigation systems to keep their crops watered. They grew corn, beans, cotton, and a few other plants native to the area. They supplemented their diet with meat from animals they hunted and with foods that grew wild, such as mesquite beans and the fruit of the saguaro cactus.

The most famous of the Hohokam settlements is Snaketown, south of present-day Phoenix, Arizona. Apparently the Hohokam were not city folk at heart—they liked to keep their distance from their neighbors. At Snaketown's peak it included only between five hundred and one thousand people, living in simple houses spread out over nearly four hundred acres.

Anthropologists—scientists who study the habits and history of human beings—have noticed that learning to make pottery is an important development in the life of a people. Societies usually first create baskets. Baskets are useful for carrying things, and they can be quite complicated and beautiful. Some peoples have even learned to cook in baskets. (They first make them watertight by coating them with pitch. Then they put heated stones into the liquid to bring it to a boil.) But pottery opens a whole new world of cooking possibilities and living arrangements.

Native Americans first created ceramic pots (made of baked clay) around

*A modern artist's view of what may have happened
to the Hohokam—their irrigation canals gone dry,
the people are abandoning their land.*

200. By 500 all the peoples of the American Southwest had mastered the art.
Pottery making was one of the tools that allowed people to settle down and
stay in one place. With pottery people could cook their food efficiently.
They could store food in case of drought and have something to eat in
wintertime, when they had no crops.

Women were the potters among the Hohokam, and they were wonderful

MAKE A SOUTHWESTERN POT

You can make a pot using the same methods as the Hohokam and other natives of the American Southwest. First, knead a ball of clay about the size of a grapefruit to warm and soften it. Break off a piece for the bottom of your pot. Shape this clay into a shallow bowl; you can either shape it with your fingers or press it over the bottom of another pot or bowl. Then, to make the sides of the bowl, break off a piece of clay about the size of a walnut and roll it between your hands to make a long strand. Wrap the strand around and on top of the base of the pot, pressing it tightly against the base layer. Keep making strands and wrapping them over the lower layers until your pot is as tall as you want. Then shape and even out the sides. To do this, the Hohokam used a tool called a paddle (you could use a tongue depressor) to shape the outside, while holding an anvil (a smooth stone is fine) on the inside.

Let your pot dry according to the directions on the clay you've used. When the pot is dry, you can paint it. The Hohokam made their brushes from the long, spiky leaves of the yucca plant, which they chewed until the fibers became soft like bristles. After you've painted your pot, bake it, with the assistance of an adult, again according to the directions. (Some kinds of clay do not need to be baked.) The Hohokam fired their pots by placing them upside down in a shallow pit lined with stones. They covered the pots with wood or animal dung and lit the fuel. As the

artists. They decorated their pots with straight lines, wavy lines, all kinds of animal figures—birds, turtles, snakes, scorpions—and lively human figures.

When you see this kind of pottery—cream-colored with red designs—you know it was made by the Hohokam. The little figures in front of the pot are effigies—vessels made to look like animals, which may have been used in burial or other religious ceremonies.

fuel burned, the pots hardened. You will probably want to fire your pot in the oven. Be careful not to touch the pot until it is completely cool.

The Hohokam apparently lived in harmony with their neighbors, the Anasazi and Mogollon. During the several hundred years their civilization lasted, they made many advances. By the early 1300s they had developed

GEE, GUYS—IT'S ONLY A GAME!

When Snaketown and other Hohokam ruins were first studied in the early 1900s, archaeologists puzzled over the large oval pits they discovered. Could these have been reservoirs for rainwater or corrals for animals? Or maybe some sort of temple? Most now agree that the pits were ball courts, dug into the earth, with sloping walls and stone markers on the floor. This idea seemed even more likely when archaeologists found figurines that looked like ballplayers, and, in one of the courts near Snaketown, two rubber balls! Ball games were evidently very popular—about two hundred Hohokam ball courts have been identified so far.

The Hohokam may have learned their ball game from the Maya, who lived to the south in Mesoamerica. The Mayan game was a cross between soccer and an all-out brawl, with the object being to keep a hard rubber ball from hitting the floor. Players scored points by knocking the ball into the opponent's "end zone." Players were allowed to use their knees, hips, and upper arms, but no feet or hands.

The Maya took their games very seriously. For them, a ball game was more a religious ceremony than a sport. Most games were designed to end in a tie, but on important ceremonial occasions, the loser was executed—either his head was chopped off or his heart cut out and offered to the gods. On the bright side, only Mayan nobles were allowed to play and it was considered an honor to be sacrificed to the gods. The Hohokam, though, appear to have been a peaceful people in many ways, and while their game was probably as rough as that played by the Maya, the losers got to go home with their heads and hearts intact.

the most extensive irrigation system on the continent, bringing water thirty miles into the desert in some places. They constructed buildings out of adobe, a sun-dried clay. Some of these buildings may have been astronomical observatories.

The name *Hohokam* means "those who have gone" in the language of the Tohono O'Odham, a people who now live where the Hohokam lived. Around 1100 Snaketown and some other large Hohokam settlements were abandoned. By 1450 the Hohokam culture had disappeared. Scientists are not sure why. Disease, drought, or conflicts with other tribes may have been the causes. Today the Tohono O'Odham and Pima peoples of the Southwest are considered the modern-day descendants of the Hohokam.

THE MAYA
DEATH OF A FOREST

In 763 Yax Pac (yash pock), not yet twenty years old, became king of the Mayan city-state of Copán. The young king knew that his kingdom was in trouble. His people were suffering from malnutrition and disease, and men had to walk many days across barren land to find firewood for their families.

Copán, in modern-day Honduras, had long been one of the Maya's most important city-states. Mayan civilization reached its greatest heights from about 250 to 900. At any given time there were many Mayan kings—and, once in a while, queens—each ruling a city-state, an independent area around a major town. In the year 800 there were probably dozens of city-states, with perhaps as many as two million people altogether. The Maya's lands stretched from the eastern coast of Mexico and the Yucatán Peninsula south to Central America, including the modern-day countries of Belize, Guatemala, El Salvador, and western Honduras.

One of the reasons the Maya flourished was that they were very clever farmers. They had learned to adapt to many different types of environments. Their homeland included high volcanic mountains, cool valleys, dense rain forests crisscrossed with swamps and rivers, and dry forest plains. The Maya developed techniques for farming in each of these different environments. They built terraces to farm the mountainsides; they filled in the swamps and rivers to create fields; and, in the forests, they slashed and burned trees, then planted their crops in the fertile ashes.

But the Maya were more than skilled farmers. Masters of knowledge and culture, they built a civilization of astonishing achievement. The Maya understood the movement of the stars and could predict eclipses with amazing accuracy. Their complex system of mathematics would not be

A huge stone ring is mounted on the wall of a Mayan ball court found on the Yucatán Peninsula. Archaeologists are not sure exactly how these rings were used in the ball games the Maya played.

equaled in Europe for centuries. They were the first civilization in the Americas to develop a complete writing system. They built great pyramids without the use of the wheel or beasts of burden. Yet these intellectual giants were also warlike and practiced some gruesome forms of human sacrifice,

This reconstructed mural from the Maya Temple of Bonampak in southern Mexico depicts a gruesome scene. Conquerors cloaked in jaguar skins stand over captives whose nails are being pulled out, leaving their fingers bloody. Another captive, perhaps already sacrificed, lies draped across the steps. The murals in this temple date from the late eighth century and were discovered by archaeologists in 1946. Recent computer-aided reconstruction is bringing them back to their original vivid color and detail.

such as offering the still-beating heart of an enemy to their gods.

Much of what we know about the Maya comes from the writings they left behind. The Maya wrote with curious-looking hieroglyphs from which strange faces and fantastic animals gaze out. Only in the last forty years or

HUGE MAYAN PALACE FOUND IN GUATEMALAN JUNGLE

Not long ago, an American archaeologist walking along a ridge in the jungles of central Guatemala fell into a hole up to his armpits. Dangling in the vegetation, he could hear snakes slithering on the ground far below. Once he pulled himself out—and stopped shaking—he realized that he had made an important discovery. He had fallen through the roof of a Mayan palace.

The archaeologist was Dr. Arthur Demarest, and in September 2000 his group of scholars announced that they had discovered an enormous royal complex in an area called Cancuén. The complex includes a 170-room palace built around eleven courtyards. The entire structure covers an area larger than two football fields. The palace was completed during the reign of a Mayan king named Tah ak Chaan, who ruled for about fifty years beginning in 740.

Archaeologists estimate that it will take at least ten years to excavate and restore the palace. They have already learned some surprising facts about what life was like in this Mayan city around the year 800. For one thing, these warlike Mayans do not seem to have been at war with anyone. Their city's power was built on trade, especially of luxury items made of jade and shiny black obsidian (glass formed by the cooling of molten lava), used for razors and knife blades. The archaeologists also found large amounts of pyrite—"fool's gold"—used for making mirrors. Apparently even the workers of Cancuén were wealthy: they had jade fillings in their teeth and were buried with expensive objects. It will be fascinating to see what else we learn as more and more of the palace is explored.

so have archaeologists learned to read Mayan hieroglyphic writing. The Maya left much for them to read, writing on shells, bones, pottery, and on paper made of fig tree bark. Only four of their bark books have survived—most were burned in the sixteenth century by a Spanish priest.

The Maya also covered their sculptures and the walls of their buildings with writing. In Copán stone carvings cover the famous Hieroglyphic Stairway. Each riser on this staircase, which originally consisted of seventy-five steps, is carved with hieroglyphs that name all the rulers of the city

The Temple of the Jaguar, rising above the rain forest, once dominated the Mayan city of Tikal. The temple was built not long before the time of Yax Pac.

and describe their exploits. Young King Yax Pac would have known the stairway well. It had been built by his father, Smoke Shell.

During the centuries before Yax Pac was born, the population of Copán had grown steadily. Food had been plentiful and the forests had supplied all the wood the people needed. By the time Yax Pac became king, at least twenty thousand people lived in or around Copán. But the growing population had taken a toll on the environment. Houses and streets had swallowed up more and more of the farmland. To make room for their fields, farmers cleared vast stretches of forest. They cut the trees from the mountainsides, leaving the rich red soil unprotected so that the hard rains easily washed it away.

Trees were cut down not only to make way for farmland but also to provide the wood needed for cooking fires and for building. Wood was used to make mortar, too. Chunks of limestone were placed atop giant wood

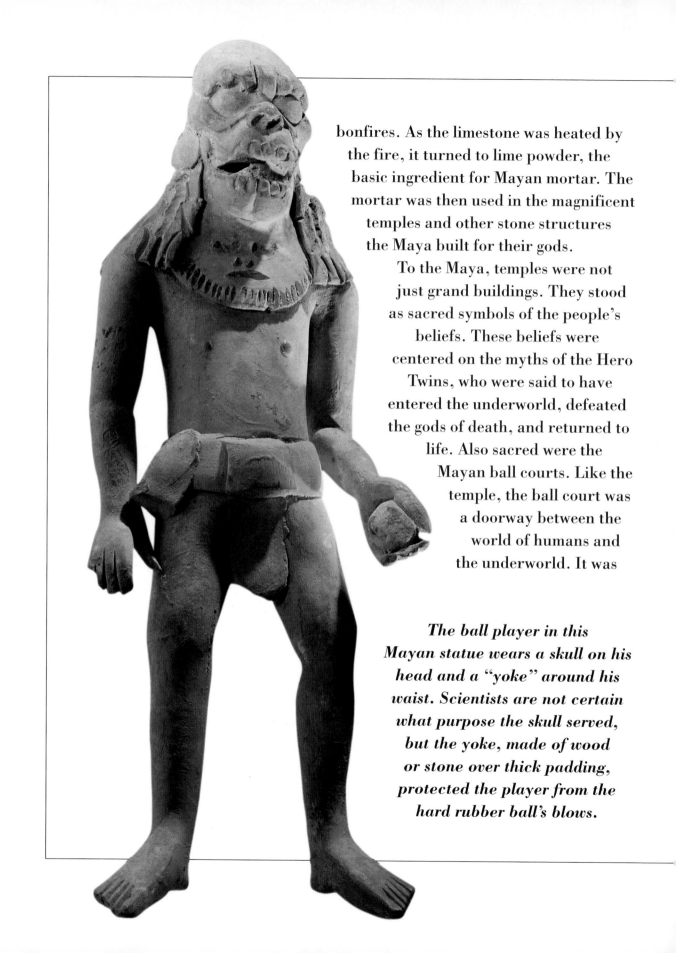

bonfires. As the limestone was heated by the fire, it turned to lime powder, the basic ingredient for Mayan mortar. The mortar was then used in the magnificent temples and other stone structures the Maya built for their gods.

To the Maya, temples were not just grand buildings. They stood as sacred symbols of the people's beliefs. These beliefs were centered on the myths of the Hero Twins, who were said to have entered the underworld, defeated the gods of death, and returned to life. Also sacred were the Mayan ball courts. Like the temple, the ball court was a doorway between the world of humans and the underworld. It was

The ball player in this Mayan statue wears a skull on his head and a "yoke" around his waist. Scientists are not certain what purpose the skull served, but the yoke, made of wood or stone over thick padding, protected the player from the hard rubber ball's blows.

The ball court at Chichén Itzá, on the Yucatán Peninsula.

in an underworld court that the Hero Twins had played ball with the gods of death and defeated them.

In his efforts to please the gods and save his people, Yax Pac built magnificent temples and one grand ball court. But even as he watched the monuments rise, he must have been haunted by thoughts of his ancestor 18 Rabbit, who had come to the throne of Copán in 695. King 18 Rabbit had built a spectacular temple and other monuments that still stood in Yax Pac's time. Nevertheless his life had ended in humiliation—he was taken captive in war and was sacrificed to the gods.

Yax Pac hoped that the gods would spare him a similar defeat, allow him to conquer his enemies, and reverse the ills that plagued his people. But great buildings were not enough. The forests continued to disappear and farmers were able to coax less and less out of the depleted land. By the last decades of Yax Pac's rule, the king no longer had the resources to build grand buildings. Yax Pac died around 820. He was the last of the great kings of Copán.

After Yax Pac, Copán remained a power for barely twenty years. Within another two hundred years, the city-state had been almost completely abandoned. Its people may have moved north to the Yucatán Peninsula, where the Maya continued to flourish until the Spanish arrived in the early 1500s. The land of Copán was so ravaged that no one could farm there again until the twentieth century.

WORLD EVENTS
AROUND 800

330—Roman emperor Constantine moves the capital to Byzantium, renaming it Constantinople
400*—Empire of Ghana in West Africa begins to establish its wealth and power
400–500—Barbarian invasions help bring the Roman Empire to an end
431—Saint Patrick arrives in Ireland
500*—Buddhism comes to Japan from China, by way of Korea
600*—Mississippian civilization takes shape in North America; the bow and arrow appears
    —The Hohokam make permanent settlements in the North American Southwest
618—Tang dynasty comes to power in China
622—Muhammad escapes from Mecca to Medina; start of the Islamic calendar
670—Kairouan founded in North Africa
711—Muslim rule is established in Spain
750—Abbasids overthrow Umayyads and become the new rulers in Baghdad
    —Mayan civilization is at its peak
752—Statue of the Buddha consecrated in Nara
755—An Lu-shan leads a rebellion against the Tang emperor Xuan-cang
756—Abd al-Rahman rules as emir of al-Andalus
763—Rebellion started by An Lu-shan in China is finally put down
    —Yax Pac becomes king of Mayan city-state of Copán
786—Harun al-Rashid becomes caliph of the Abbasids; he will rule until 809
793—Lindisfarne is ravaged by the Vikings
794—Japanese emperor moves capital to Kyoto
797—Irene takes the title of empress of the Byzantines
800—Charlemagne is crowned Roman emperor
802—Nicephorus I deposes Irene and becomes Byzantine emperor
814—Charlemagne dies
900*—Beginning of monumental building in Mississippian city of Cahokia
907—Tang dynasty comes to an end
1000*—Leif Eriksson and the Vikings reach Newfoundland
1066—William the Conqueror of Normandy takes the throne in England
1076—Muslim Berbers invade the empire of Ghana and capture the capital, Kumbi Salih
1100*—Snaketown is abandoned
1400*—Cahokia abandoned
1492—Muslims are expelled from Spain by Ferdinand and Isabella

*dates approximate

GLOSSARY

Abbasids (uh-BAH-sids) members of the dynasty that ruled the Islamic empire from 750 to 1258, from their capital in Baghdad

al-Andalus Arabic name for the area of Spain ruled by Muslims from the early 700s until 1492

Angles a Germanic people who, along with the Saxons and Jutes, invaded England in the fifth century

anthropologist a scientist who studies human society, either past or present

archaeologist someone who studies the past by examining the material remains of a culture

Berbers native peoples of North Africa

brazier a container that holds burning coals or other fuel used for heating

caliph (KAY-lif) political and spiritual leader of Islam

caravan a group of travelers and their pack animals who journey together for reasons of safety, as across a desert

Celts (kelts) tribal groups once dominant in much of Europe; today people of Celtic descent live primarily in Scotland, Wales, Ireland, and Brittany

clan a group of people who are related through a common relative in the distant past

dynasty a series of rulers who belong to the same family

equinoxes the two times during the year when the sun crosses the equator and day and night are the same length

Franks a people who lived in present-day France and Germany during the Middle Ages

Hegira (hih-JEE-rah) the escape of the Prophet Muhammad from Mecca to Medina in 622; this event marks the beginning of the Islamic calendar

Islam the religion of Muslims, who believe that Allah is the one God and Muhammad is his prophet

Lombards Germanic people who invaded northern Italy in the sixth century and established a kingdom there

manuscript a book that is written out, illustrated, and bound by hand

missionary a person who travels to a far-off place to teach his or her religion to the people of that place

mosque a Muslim place of worship

muezzin (moo-EH-zen) a Muslim crier who sings out the call to prayer from the mosque five times a day

Muslim a follower of the religion of Islam

nomads people who move from place to place in search of food for themselves and their animals

Normans the Vikings, or Norsemen, who settled in northwest France in the tenth century and conquered England in 1066

pagan believing in many gods

papyrus a paperlike writing material made from the stems of a grassy plant that grows in wet areas of North Africa and southern Europe

parchment a sheet for writing made from the skin of a goat or sheep

prehistoric relating to times before written history

prophet a person who is believed to speak the word of God

Saxons a Germanic people who, along with the Angles and Jutes, invaded England in the fifth century

scribe someone who copies manuscripts or other documents by hand

terrace a flat area created on a hillside or mountainside, usually for farming

Umayyads (oo-MY-ids) members of the dynasty that ruled the Islamic empire from 661 to 750, from their capital in Damascus

Visigoths members of a Germanic tribe that invaded the Roman Empire in the fourth century and settled in France and Spain

For Further Reading

Editors of Time-Life Books. *TimeFrame AD 800–1000: Fury of the Northmen.* Alexandria, VA: Time-Life Books, 1988. An appealing book filled with unusual illustrations. Includes interesting and informative essays on the Vikings, the Byzantine Empire, the Japanese, and the Americas.

Fisher, Leonard Everett. *Gods and Goddesses of the Ancient Maya.* New York: Holiday House, 1999. A colorful picture book. Simplified but useful.

Galvin, Irene Flum. *The Ancient Maya.* New York: Marshall Cavendish, 1997. An excellent overview of Mayan civilization. Beautifully illustrated. Includes a time line.

George, Linda S. *The Golden Age of Islam.* New York: Marshall Cavendish, 1998. A history of the arts and culture of Islam, especially during the era of unprecedented splendor when the Abbasids ruled, in the eighth through thirteenth centuries. Many colorful illustrations.

Guy, John. *Viking Life.* Hauppauge, NY: Barron's, 1998. Brief, easy-to-read overview with lots of drawings and photos.

Hitti, Philip K. *The Arabs: A Short History.* Chicago: Gateway Editions, 1985. A good basic text. Interesting sections on Charlemagne, Harun al-Rashid, and Islamic Spain.

Iseminger, William R. "Mighty Cahokia." *Archaeology,* May/June 1996. Written by the curator of the Cahokia Mounds State Historic Site. Gives detailed information and drawings and color photographs of the site.

Millar, Heather. *China's Tang Dynasty.* New York: Marshall Cavendish, 1996. A good overview of this important period, written in a lively, engaging style.

Vesilind, Priit J. "In Search of Vikings." *National Geographic* 197, no. 5 (May 2000).

ON-LINE INFORMATION*

www.africana.com
A wealth of information relating to
Africa and African Americans. Includes
articles on ancient African civilizations.

www.columbia.edu/itc/ealac/V3613/kyoto
The history of the Japanese city of Kyoto,
with diagrams, paintings, and photos.

www.fordham.edu/halsall/source/1000bag
hdad.html
Wonderful selection from the Arab
historian and geographer al-Yakut, who
wrote around the year 1200, describing
the city of Baghdad in its glory.

www.humnet.ucla.edu/santiago/hist
chrl.html
A lively history of Charlemagne and his
achievements. Includes medieval legends
about him.

www.medicine.wustl.edu/~kellerk/
cahokia.html
Site maintained by the Cahokia Mounds
State Historic Site. Includes pictures and
a detailed history.

www.pbs.org/wgbh/nova/vikings
From this site you can explore a Viking
village, learn secrets of Norse ships, and
find out about dendrochronology (tree
ring dating).

www.westafricanjourney.com
Information on the empire of Ghana
and other ancient African empires.
Also includes pages on modern life in
West Africa.

www.destination360.com/tikal/guide.htm
A virtual tour of the ruins of the ancient
Mayan city of Tikal, in Guatemala.
Includes photos, maps, pictures of
artifacts, and a section on Mayan culture.

*Websites change from time to time. For
additional on-line information, check with
the media specialist at your local library.*

ABOUT THE AUTHOR
Linda S. George has taught Middle East
history and literature at Columbia
University in New York and at Drew
University in Madison, New Jersey. She
has a Ph.D. from Harvard University in
linguistics and wrote her dissertation on
Arabic language change and storytelling
in the *Thousand and One Nights*. Ms.
George has lived and studied in many
parts of the Middle East, including Egypt
and Morocco. This is her third book for
Benchmark Books. She lives in New Jersey
with her husband, Richard, and their son,
Alexander.

INDEX